This Planner Belong To:

Quick Links

Profile

Schedule

Month/Weeks/Days

Project

Reflection

Notes

🔗 Days

1 2 3 4 5 6 7 8 9 10 11 12 13
14 15 16 17 18 19 20 21 22 23
24 25 26 27 28 29 30 31

Profile

DETAILS

NAME

DATE OF BIRTH

COUNTRY

GRADE

YEAR

PHONE

ADDRESS

HOBBIES & INTERESTS

MY SMART GOALS

What do you want to accomplish?

S
SPECIFIC

How will you keep track of your progress?

M
MEASURABLE

What do you need to do in order to reach the goal?

A
ACTIONABLE

How will this goal help you?

R
RELEVANT

When will you accomplish this goal?

T
TIMELY

Write down your SMART goal.

BIRTHDAYS

January	February	March
April	May	June
July	August	September
October	November	December

Important Dates

PROFESSIONAL LEARNING

Title	Description

SELF-CARE CHALLENGE

Schedule

SCHEDULE

TIME	MON	TUE	WED	THU	FRI	SAT	SUN

IMPORTANT

Month

MONTHLY PLANNER

MONTH / YEAR: --------------------

	Mon	Tue	wed	Thu	Fri	Sat	Sun
WEEK1							
WEEK2							
WEEK3							
WEEK4							
WEEK5							

EVENTS

NOTES

Weeks

WEEK -- PLANNER

□ Date: _______________________

Goals of the Week	**Monday**
Top Priorities	**Tuesday**
Reflection	**Wednesday**
	Thursday
To-Do List	**Friday**
✐ **Notes**	**Saturday**
	Sunday

WEEK -- PLANNER

📅 Date: _______________________

Goals of the Week

Top Priorities

Reflection

To-Do List

📝 **Notes**

Monday

Tuesday

Wednesday

Thursday

Friday

Saturday

Sunday

WEEK -- PLANNER

☐ Date: _______________________

Goals of the Week	**Monday**
Top Priorities	**Tuesday**
Reflection	**Wednesday**
	Thursday
To-Do List	**Friday**
☑ **Notes**	**Saturday**
	Sunday

WEEK -- PLANNER

📅 Date: _______________________

Goals of the Week

Top Priorities

Reflection

To-Do List

📝 Notes

Monday

Tuesday

Wednesday

Thursday

Friday

Saturday

Sunday

WEEK -- PLANNER

📅 Date: ____________________

Goals of the Week	**Monday**
Top Priorities	**Tuesday**
Reflection	**Wednesday**
	Thursday
To-Do List	**Friday**
📝 **Notes**	**Saturday**
	Sunday

Days

DAY -- PLANNER

DATE: ___________________

TODAY'S SCHEDULE

6 am:

7 am:

8 am:

9 am:

10 am:

11 am:

12 am:

1 pm:

2 pm:

3 pm:

4 pm:

5 pm:

6 pm:

7 pm:

8 pm:

9 pm:

TASKS

REFLECTION

NOTES

DAY -- PLANNER

DATE: ___________________

TODAY'S SCHEDULE

6 am:

7 am:

8 am:

9 am:

10 am:

11 am:

12 am:

1 pm:

2 pm:

3 pm:

4 pm:

5 pm:

6 pm:

7 pm:

8 pm:

9 pm:

TASKS

REFLECTION

NOTES

DAY -- PLANNER

DATE: ________________________

TODAY'S SCHEDULE

6 am:

7 am:

8 am:

9 am:

10 am:

11 am:

12 am:

1 pm:

2 pm:

3 pm:

4 pm:

5 pm:

6 pm:

7 pm:

8 pm:

9 pm:

TASKS

REFLECTION

NOTES

DAY -- PLANNER

DATE: _______________________

TODAY'S SCHEDULE

6 am:

7 am:

8 am:

9 am:

10 am:

11 am:

12 am:

1 pm:

2 pm:

3 pm:

4 pm:

5 pm:

6 pm:

7 pm:

8 pm:

9 pm:

TASKS

REFLECTION

NOTES

DAY -- PLANNER

DATE: ________________________

TODAY'S SCHEDULE

6 am:

7 am:

8 am:

9 am:

10 am:

11 am:

12 am:

1 pm:

2 pm:

3 pm:

4 pm:

5 pm:

6 pm:

7 pm:

8 pm:

9 pm:

TASKS

REFLECTION

NOTES

DAY -- PLANNER

DATE: _______________________

TODAY'S SCHEDULE

6 am:

7 am:

8 am:

9 am:

10 am:

11 am:

12 am:

1 pm:

2 pm:

3 pm:

4 pm:

5 pm:

6 pm:

7 pm:

8 pm:

9 pm:

TASKS

REFLECTION

NOTES

DAY -- PLANNER

DATE: ___________________

TODAY'S SCHEDULE

6 am:

7 am:

8 am:

9 am:

10 am:

11 am:

12 am:

1 pm:

2 pm:

3 pm:

4 pm:

5 pm:

6 pm:

7 pm:

8 pm:

9 pm:

TASKS

REFLECTION

NOTES

DAY -- PLANNER

DATE: _______________________

TODAY'S SCHEDULE

6 am:

7 am:

8 am:

9 am:

10 am:

11 am:

12 am:

1 pm:

2 pm:

3 pm:

4 pm:

5 pm:

6 pm:

7 pm:

8 pm:

9 pm:

TASKS

REFLECTION

NOTES

DAY -- PLANNER

DATE: ________________________

TODAY'S SCHEDULE

6 am:

7 am:

8 am:

9 am:

10 am:

11 am:

12 am:

1 pm:

2 pm:

3 pm:

4 pm:

5 pm:

6 pm:

7 pm:

8 pm:

9 pm:

TASKS

REFLECTION

NOTES

DAY -- PLANNER

DATE: _____________________

TODAY'S SCHEDULE

6 am:

7 am:

8 am:

9 am:

10 am:

11 am:

12 am:

1 pm:

2 pm:

3 pm:

4 pm:

5 pm:

6 pm:

7 pm:

8 pm:

9 pm:

TASKS

REFLECTION

NOTES

DAY -- PLANNER

DATE: ___________________

TODAY'S SCHEDULE

6 am:

7 am:

8 am:

9 am:

10 am:

11 am:

12 am:

1 pm:

2 pm:

3 pm:

4 pm:

5 pm:

6 pm:

7 pm:

8 pm:

9 pm:

TASKS

REFLECTION

NOTES

DAY -- PLANNER

DATE: ________________________

TODAY'S SCHEDULE

6 am:

7 am:

8 am:

9 am:

10 am:

11 am:

12 am:

1 pm:

2 pm:

3 pm:

4 pm:

5 pm:

6 pm:

7 pm:

8 pm:

9 pm:

TASKS

REFLECTION

NOTES

DAY -- PLANNER

DATE: _______________________

TODAY'S SCHEDULE

6 am:

7 am:

8 am:

9 am:

10 am:

11 am:

12 am:

1 pm:

2 pm:

3 pm:

4 pm:

5 pm:

6 pm:

7 pm:

8 pm:

9 pm:

TASKS

REFLECTION

NOTES

DAY -- PLANNER

DATE: ________________________

TODAY'S SCHEDULE

6 am:

7 am:

8 am:

9 am:

10 am:

11 am:

12 am:

1 pm:

2 pm:

3 pm:

4 pm:

5 pm:

6 pm:

7 pm:

8 pm:

9 pm:

TASKS

REFLECTION

NOTES

DAY -- PLANNER

DATE: ________________________

TODAY'S SCHEDULE

6 am:

7 am:

8 am:

9 am:

10 am:

11 am:

12 am:

1 pm:

2 pm:

3 pm:

4 pm:

5 pm:

6 pm:

7 pm:

8 pm:

9 pm:

TASKS

REFLECTION

NOTES

DAY -- PLANNER

DATE: ________________________

TODAY'S SCHEDULE

6 am:

7 am:

8 am:

9 am:

10 am:

11 am:

12 am:

1 pm:

2 pm:

3 pm:

4 pm:

5 pm:

6 pm:

7 pm:

8 pm:

9 pm:

TASKS

REFLECTION

NOTES

DAY -- PLANNER

DATE: ___________________

TODAY'S SCHEDULE

6 am:

7 am:

8 am:

9 am:

10 am:

11 am:

12 am:

1 pm:

2 pm:

3 pm:

4 pm:

5 pm:

6 pm:

7 pm:

8 pm:

9 pm:

TASKS

REFLECTION

NOTES

DAY -- PLANNER

DATE: ___________________

TODAY'S SCHEDULE

6 am:

7 am:

8 am:

9 am:

10 am:

11 am:

12 am:

1 pm:

2 pm:

3 pm:

4 pm:

5 pm:

6 pm:

7 pm:

8 pm:

9 pm:

TASKS

REFLECTION

NOTES

DAY -- PLANNER

DATE: _______________________

TODAY'S SCHEDULE

6 am:

7 am:

8 am:

9 am:

10 am:

11 am:

12 am:

1 pm:

2 pm:

3 pm:

4 pm:

5 pm:

6 pm:

7 pm:

8 pm:

9 pm:

TASKS

REFLECTION

NOTES

DAY -- PLANNER

DATE: ___________________

TODAY'S SCHEDULE

6 am:

7 am:

8 am:

9 am:

10 am:

11 am:

12 am:

1 pm:

2 pm:

3 pm:

4 pm:

5 pm:

6 pm:

7 pm:

8 pm:

9 pm:

TASKS

REFLECTION

NOTES

DAY -- PLANNER

DATE: ___________________

<table>
<tr><td>

TODAY'S SCHEDULE

6 am:

7 am:

8 am:

9 am:

10 am:

11 am:

12 am:

1 pm:

2 pm:

3 pm:

4 pm:

5 pm:

6 pm:

7 pm:

8 pm:

9 pm:

</td><td>

TASKS

</td></tr>
</table>

REFLECTION

NOTES

DAY -- PLANNER

DATE: ________________________

TODAY'S SCHEDULE

6 am:

7 am:

8 am:

9 am:

10 am:

11 am:

12 am:

1 pm:

2 pm:

3 pm:

4 pm:

5 pm:

6 pm:

7 pm:

8 pm:

9 pm:

TASKS

REFLECTION

NOTES

DAY -- PLANNER

DATE: _______________________

TODAY'S SCHEDULE

6 am:

7 am:

8 am:

9 am:

10 am:

11 am:

12 am:

1 pm:

2 pm:

3 pm:

4 pm:

5 pm:

6 pm:

7 pm:

8 pm:

9 pm:

TASKS

REFLECTION

NOTES

DAY -- PLANNER

DATE: _______________________

TODAY'S SCHEDULE

6 am:

7 am:

8 am:

9 am:

10 am:

11 am:

12 am:

1 pm:

2 pm:

3 pm:

4 pm:

5 pm:

6 pm:

7 pm:

8 pm:

9 pm:

TASKS

REFLECTION

NOTES

DAY -- PLANNER

DATE: _____________________

TODAY'S SCHEDULE

6 am:

7 am:

8 am:

9 am:

10 am:

11 am:

12 am:

1 pm:

2 pm:

3 pm:

4 pm:

5 pm:

6 pm:

7 pm:

8 pm:

9 pm:

TASKS

REFLECTION

NOTES

DAY -- PLANNER

DATE: ___________________

TODAY'S SCHEDULE

6 am:

7 am:

8 am:

9 am:

10 am:

11 am:

12 am:

1 pm:

2 pm:

3 pm:

4 pm:

5 pm:

6 pm:

7 pm:

8 pm:

9 pm:

TASKS

REFLECTION

NOTES

DAY -- PLANNER

DATE: _______________________

TODAY'S SCHEDULE

6 am:

7 am:

8 am:

9 am:

10 am:

11 am:

12 am:

1 pm:

2 pm:

3 pm:

4 pm:

5 pm:

6 pm:

7 pm:

8 pm:

9 pm:

TASKS

REFLECTION

NOTES

DAY -- PLANNER

DATE: _______________________

TODAY'S SCHEDULE

6 am:

7 am:

8 am:

9 am:

10 am:

11 am:

12 am:

1 pm:

2 pm:

3 pm:

4 pm:

5 pm:

6 pm:

7 pm:

8 pm:

9 pm:

TASKS

REFLECTION

NOTES

DAY -- PLANNER

DATE: ___________________

TODAY'S SCHEDULE

6 am:

7 am:

8 am:

9 am:

10 am:

11 am:

12 am:

1 pm:

2 pm:

3 pm:

4 pm:

5 pm:

6 pm:

7 pm:

8 pm:

9 pm:

TASKS

REFLECTION

NOTES

DAY -- PLANNER

DATE: _________________________

TODAY'S SCHEDULE

6 am:

7 am:

8 am:

9 am:

10 am:

11 am:

12 am:

1 pm:

2 pm:

3 pm:

4 pm:

5 pm:

6 pm:

7 pm:

8 pm:

9 pm:

TASKS

REFLECTION

NOTES

DAY -- PLANNER

DATE: _______________________

TODAY'S SCHEDULE

6 am:

7 am:

8 am:

9 am:

10 am:

11 am:

12 am:

1 pm:

2 pm:

3 pm:

4 pm:

5 pm:

6 pm:

7 pm:

8 pm:

9 pm:

TASKS

REFLECTION

NOTES

Project

MONTHLY PROJECT

START DATE: _______________________ DUE DATE: _______________

MEMBERS	RESOURCES	COMPLETION

TIME LINE: ____

PROJECT DESCRIPTION

ACTION PLAN

PROJECT NOTES

Reflection

MONTHLY REFLECTION

This Month In one word

Challenges

Highlight

What can I do to improve next month

Personal Growth
Money
Healthy
Goals

Notes

SCHOOL NOTES

Date:------------

SCHOOL NOTES

Date:------------

SCHOOL NOTES

Date:------------

END